THE ASPIRING MINIMALIST

By H. FARIZI

COPYRIGHT DISCLAIMER

WORDS FROM THE AUTHOR

Hello! I'm HASH. I'm a Film Director and as you probably are, I'm also an aspiring minimalist. Minimalism Knowledge is like a hole I can never fully fill, explains why I'll forever be an "aspiring" minimalist. To be honest I was never one but for the past few years, I took the leap and jumped slowly into Minimalism. It changed my life 10x to the better, I'm happier and closer to my career goal more than ever. In this book, lies the resources and information I've tried and implemented that got me here today.

Happy Decluttering!

CONTENTS

INTRODUCTION

Minimalism, as a lifestyle, grabs characteristics from minimalism as a type of artistry and design. A repeating theme of anything minimal is that it is reduced to its center components. Anything that isn't vital for the book to act as what it should do is viewed as a bit much.

Regardless of whether it be composing, lofts, furniture, clothing, bicycles, music, cell phones, or autos, minimalism is a development making strides in numerous territories of current life.

Many people are, at any rate, fairly acquainted with the term 'minimalist workmanship,' which will evoke in a great many people's psyches what has all the earmarks of being essential craftsmanship, for the most part utilizing beautiful hues with little detail.

From a customer stance, from various perspectives, minimalism, as a lifestyle, has a strong fondness with green development. Overabundance is avoided, and only what is fundamental is required to satisfy the target.

For example, a minimal pair of tennis shoes may exclude marking and other physical impacts that don't add to the general shoe's capacity. A minimal kitchen will only comprise utensils that are typically utilized and won't highlight things that are only here and there or never employed.

One prominent instance of minimalism that has moved toward becoming standard in the present culture is the physical design of Apple's well-known iPod, notwithstanding the iPhone. While gradually including more, Google's home page would likewise be viewed as a success for minimalism (compared to Yahoo's home page).

Obviously, precisely what minimal is and what it isn't is a crucial discussion of minimalists. Anyway, the critical objectives of minimalism are commonly shared by all who are into the development.

With the approach of the web, individuals who look for a progressively minimal lifestyle can utilize the internet as an incredible asset to help design their lives. Be it the numerous minimalism related websites on the web, to the capacity to painstakingly inquire about items online of internet business stores, to the web index's ability to help discover anything minimalism related.

Minimalism in purchased items is a consistently changing field that appears to keep pace with the quick advances in innovation. It demonstrates that individuals favor less complicated articles and apparatuses.

CHAPTER ONE

Top 8 Benefits of Living A Minimalist Lifestyle

Minimalism is an approach to put a stop to the greed of our general surroundings. It's the inverse of each commercial we see on the radio and TV. We live in a general public that prides itself on the collection of stuff; we gobble up commercialization, material possessions, mess, obligation, diversions, and clamor.

What we don't appear to have is any significance left in our reality.

By embracing a minimalist lifestyle, you can toss out what you don't need to focus on what you do need.

I know how little we need to survive. I was sufficiently lucky to live in a van for four months while going all through Australia. This experience taught me important exercises about the main thing and how little we truly need all the stuff we encircle ourselves with.

Toning it down would be best.

Carrying on with a minimalist lifestyle is reducing. There are a couple of clear benefits of minimalism, for example, less cleaning and stress, a progressively sorted out family unit, and more money to be found, yet there are additionally a couple of profound, life-evolving benefits.

What we don't usually acknowledge is that, when we reduce, we reduce more than just stuff.

Think about only a portion of the benefits of living with fewer possessions:

1. Create space for what's vital

When we cleanse our garbage drawers and wardrobes, we create space and harmony. We lose that claustrophobic inclination, and we can inhale once more. Create the space to top off our lives with importance rather than stuff.

2. More opportunity

The amassing of stuff resembles a grapple; it secures us. We are alarmed continuously of losing all our 'stuff.' Release it, and you will encounter an opportunity: an opportunity to escape from ravenousness, obligation, fixation, and workaholic behavior.

3. Focus on wellbeing and pastimes

When you invest less energy at Home Depot attempting fruitlessly to stay ahead of the Joneses, you create an opening to do the things you love, things that you never appeared to possess the energy to do.

Everybody is continually saying they don't have enough time, yet how many people genuinely stop and take a gander at what they are investing their energy doing?

You could be getting a charge out of a multi-day with your children, hitting up the rec center, rehearsing yoga, perusing a decent book, or voyaging. Whatever it is that you love, you could be doing; however, instead you are stuck at Sears looking for more stuff.

4. Less focus on material possessions

All the stuff we encircle ourselves with is just a diversion, and we are filling a void. Money can't purchase happiness. However, it can buy comfort. After the underlying solace is fulfilled, that is the place our fixation on money should end.

We are barraged by the media, exhibiting guarantees of happiness through material measures. It's no big surprise we battle it regularly. Oppose those inclinations. It's an unfulfilled way, and it won't fulfill you.

It's hard not to get stuck in the industrialism trap. I need consistent updates that it's a misguided feeling of happiness. I appreciate stuff, yet I likewise perceive that I needn't bother with it.

5. More significant serenity

When we stick to material possessions, we create pressure since we are always terrified of losing these things. By disentangling your life, you can lose your connection to these things and eventually create a quiet, serene personality.

The fewer things you need to stress over, the more harmony you have, and it's as necessary as that.

6. More happiness

When de-jumbling your life, happiness comes typically since you float towards the things that matter most. You see the bogus guarantees in all the messiness unmistakably; it resembles a broken shield against life's actual pith.

You will likewise discover happiness in being increasingly productive, and you will find fixation by having refocused your needs. You will discover euphoria by getting a charge out of backing off.

7. Less fear of disappointment

When you take a gander at Buddhist priests, they have no fear, and they do not doubt since they don't have anything to lose.

In whatever you wish to seek, you can exceed expectations if you aren't tormented with the fear of losing all your common possessions. You have to figure out how to put a rooftop over your head, yet also realize that you have little to fear except fear itself.

8. More Certainty

The whole minimalist lifestyle advances distinction and confidence. This will make you increasingly sure about your quest for happiness.

5 Ways Your Mental Health Will Benefit from Minimalism

Minimalism has turned into somewhat of a contemporary expression of late. As we live more mindfully, it is normal to assess what we have.

When we are never again just making a cursory effort in our day by day lives, we start to ponder the items that encompass us in our homes. We understand the amount we need and the amount we don't.

What Is Minimalism?

It is tied in with finding what is imperative.

Taking a mental stock of our belongings and choosing what improves our lives and what does not is the initial move toward a progressively minimalist lifestyle.

When we have freed ourselves of every one of those additional belongings that are hindering us, we have the chance to accomplish the minimalist life-style.

Minimalism and Mental Illness

In any case, minimalism isn't only an idea that causes us to rearrange our homes and lives in a progressively compelling and stylishly satisfying way.

Minimalism can be a useful way to battle mental illness of all degrees of seriousness, from uneasiness to schizophrenia and more.

By having fewer things to occupy or trigger you, your mental health will be affected. Minimalism allows you to block out all the commotion in your life and make improvements.

Here are five ways moderation is right for your mental health.
1. Harmony and Clarity

Cleaning up your living and additional office space, you are doing likewise for your mind. Minimalist conditions are peaceful, permitting us not to be overstimulated.

Overstimulation is an adversary of mindfulness, as one can't think clearly when we are overwhelmed with physical data.

Besides, a bounty of upgrades jumbling up our homes or workplaces implies there are a lot of visual cues that can trigger considerations or recollections. And keeping in mind that that isn't a terrible thing, it tends to be damnation for somebody managing mental illness.

Overstimulation brought about by an excessive amount of "stuff" may significantly trigger schizophrenic scenes in somebody that is inclined to them.

In this manner, a minimalist methodology facilitates this issue and clears a path for a life of harmony and purity.

2. A Step Toward Self-Discovery

Even though disposing of a large measure of your material possessions will appear as though you're losing a piece of you, it's only a step in finding yourself.

At the point when there are never again such vast numbers of things around to occupy you from who you genuinely are, the most illuminating and original self-revelation happens.

Keeping your mind occupied with pointless things may appear to be an excellent way to adapt to mental illness. However, it is temporary.

Over the long haul, knowing your identity is the best thing you can accomplish for yourself.

Attention to your actual self will help you on your way to recuperation since it will give you the essential fuel to continue.

3. Concentrate on What Is Important

When you have less stuff, you have fewer diversions. It is so natural to lose focus when reminded of different things you could or should be doing.

With the opportunity to focus, you start to expel the internal mess from your mind.

You have the alternative to discover a place in your home in which you never again feel torn in twelve distinct ways, which will do something unusual for your mental health.

This focus could be utilized to pick up something or offer something. It may be used to compose a book or gain proficiency with another dialect, giving you a feeling of pride and achievement that will saturate into different everyday issues.

Having sufficient energy, space, and focus important for such an achievement can push you along your way toward a progressively peaceful life.

Also, by blocking out the commotion and focusing on what is vital, before long, you will acknowledge the main thing and what is not.

Expelling yourself from circumstances that are not useful to you can be extremely recuperating, and it will help you reconnect with yourself on a more profound dimension.

4. More Space to Unwind

By ridding your living zone of an unneeded mess, you make open space.

Instinctively, the more open space, the more peaceful and less choking it feels, and there is some proof to propose that the human mind is affected by the separation between items.

In this way, making your home feel progressively extensive is probably going to be valuable for your mental health.

The home will turn into a plain canvas, where you loosen up in the way you see fit, rather than dealing with your various belongings day by day.

There is an opportunity to do what you need with this space. Your home or own corner could turn into a place of imagination for painting or gardening.

As indicated by one investigation, making craftsmanship decreases cortisol levels, which is one hormone that adds to pressure, nervousness, and numerous other mental illnesses.

Utilizing that space to accomplish something pleasant additionally discharges endorphins, the synthetic substances in the mind that makes us feel better.

Rather than having visual cues surrounding you, those undesirable trigger musings, it's smarter to make something new.

Also, communicating in creative ways may enable you to recuperate from the deep lows of mental conditions, for example, tension and despair.

5. An Exercise in Self-Control

Owning a lot of material goods is unimaginably enticing, which is the reason many of us fall into industrialism so effectively.

Along these lines, changing from a jumbled and materialistic lifestyle toward the refreshing straightforwardness of minimalism is a great choice to make.

In any case, if you choose to go down that road, you won't just be more settled, but also more in control of your own life.

This is even more essential if you are battling mental illness.

An enormous piece of mental illness is feeling a loss of control over different, if not all, parts of your life. Anybody realizes how discouraging this issue is and how it can send you spiraling.

This is the motivation behind why recapturing control over probably a few parts of your life is significant for you.

That is not all. By not focusing your consideration on material possessions, for example, too many cool garments or another vehicle that you don't generally require, you can confront your issues successfully.

There will never again be any diversions that enable you to redirect from what you ought to have been recognizing from the start. Realizing what's overloading you is the most critical step toward effectively adapting to it.

How Can You Achieve Minimalism In Corporate For A Healthy Lifestyle?

Minimalism gives incalculable advantages. In a short sentence, minimalism intends to perform an assignment in a certifiable and least painful way. A minimalist methodology is advantageous to improve health and fitness as it gets an incredible decrease in pressure. This methodology is most pivotal at this timeframe because people have built a wrong idea about health and wellness. They spend large measures of cash and time on destructive weight control plans, rec center enrollments, and perilous enhancements because of the impact of media and advertisers. They begin to trust that they can't be healthy without experiencing these entangled procedures. It's not valid. Following a minimalist way, we can improve our health and personal satisfaction.

As we just began with the New Year, we've been besieged with messages, considerations, and proposals about washed down, convenient solutions and tricks. You ought to keep away from them no matter what and instead grasp the minimalist strategy for better health to remain healthy. Here are a few hints to use minimalism:

1. Move it as you can

A mandatory workout and going to an exercise center to perform bodyweight workouts isn't vital. You can do them at home before getting down to business or after work. Take advantage of going from home to work. Your cycle is hanging tight for you. Take it to achieve your work. Also, what you do isn't essential unless it is reliable. You have to move your body no less than 20-30 minutes consistently. Keep in mind there are unlimited conceivable outcomes. Search for neighborhood stops in your general vicinity or wander without agonizing where it will take you.

2. Eat Real food

You should expend food as crisp as could be allowed. A straightforward eating regimen with whole natural foods, like organic products, vegetables, nuts, and seeds, is the extraordinary aide to reboot your health. You can eat such healthy food in little time while working. Most people think dairy food is the best to have supplements; however, they are wrong. Dairy foods can cause sinusitis and hypersensitivities if not acknowledged by your body. So it's smarter to devour them if your body is good with such foods. Current bundled food or comfort foods are loaded with an additive to broaden their everyday life. To avoid such foods, utilize a minimalist way and go natural. Try not to stress that you have to forfeit everything delectable and delicious. You can, in any case, make the most of your favorite, unhealthy food on occasions like birthdays, commemorations, holidays, and different events without pointless blame. It ought to be every so often.

3. Get rest

Offering rest to your body after a full move of work is essential to accomplish significant serenity. In a work culture fixated on completing however much as could be expected in the littlest measure of time, rest has turned into a word synonymous with apathetic. You have to rest each day in the wake of originating from work. You can rest all Sunday without doing exercise. Much the same as a day for rest, the following vital thing is to take a sans screen day. Release every electronic gadget, feel your internal harmony, and appreciate the rapture. By Monday, your body and mind will be invigorated to get back to work.

4. Minimalism is the freedom from trickery

Even though nobody purposefully picks it, a great many people live in trickery. They live one life around their family or companions, one life around their colleagues, and another life around their neighbors. Such lifestyle expects them to speak to a specific outer picture subordinate to their circumstances. Therefore, it pressurizes their minds to go the additional mile and perform double lifestyles. Then again, an honest life is uniform and steady. This lifestyle is transferable and adaptable regardless of the circumstance. In a minimalist way, it is similarly conducted on Friday evening for what it's worth on Sunday morning... for what it's worth on Monday morning. It is reliable, trustworthy, and familiar. It works in all conditions, and it's the best lifestyle that gives you full freedom to overhaul your abilities.

5. Give yourself some time

Our lives are speeding at a rapid pace. Everybody is excessively rushed, excessively hurried, and overly focused. We work invariably long for quite a long time to pay the bills, however, fall further into obligations. We surge starting with one action then onto the next—performing various tasks en route—yet never appear to complete everything. We stay inconsistently associated with people through our PDAs, yet obvious life-changing connections keep getting away from us.

Minimalism backs life off and liberates us from this cutting-edge frenzy to live quicker. It gives you the freedom to withdraw. It tries to keep just the fundamentals and overlook the phony things. It expels the false people from our lives and maintains critical things. Also, in doing as such, it increases the value of our lives.

All in all, minimalism decidedly impacts each part of our life whether it is close to home or expert. Following these tips, you can be a healthier minimalist. Minimalism conveys an incentive to your life and makes it authentic, like an unadulterated and recently arranged Windows 7 PC. No messes, no impermanent documents, and no infections. Moreover, a pure mind, soul, and body are the fundamentals for the most joyful life.

How Minimalism Can Benefit Your Mental Health

Moderation may feel like merely one more usual fashion. However, it's one that has got some sudden advantages. Dissimilar to different trends that appear as endeavors to get you to purchase increasingly, progressively more, moderation can profit your mental health. Its accentuation on less can give you (and your wallet) somewhat of a break. Here are five reasons you should give this trend a try.

Less Clutter Helps Declutter Your Brain

Less clutter around you isn't merely attractive. It's useful for your cerebrum, as well. It encourages you to concentrate since clutter is diverting. It essentially makes your mind perform multiple tasks the whole time you're attempting to work, so a cleaner region will enable you to concentrate on whatever you're doing. This causes you to achieve more, while letting go of the things you don't need to consider right now. Cluttered space, cluttered personality; however, clear space, clear personality!

Needing Less Versus Needing Less

By setting out on an adventure of moderation, you still have to get all the things you need. It is anything but a path to poverty or to doing without. It is, however, a path to enable you to become familiar with the contrast between the things you need and the things you don't need. When you become acclimated to it, you'll feel less influenced to rival everyone, purchasing stuff you don't need. Like this, you'll feel less on edge about your place in life and if you're "keeping up with the Jones'."

Give Yourself Freedom

If you somehow managed to haul out all of your effects, you'd most likely be stunned at precisely how many things you possess. All of those things attach you to something, even if it's only a dream you had for yourself. Disposing of the overabundance (not everything, just the abundance) will be a weight off your home, your funds, and your psyche. You'll be beginning sans preparation—or if nothing else from what you are as of now, without all the desires you've made for yourself.

That prompts an unexpected burst of opportunity and inventiveness. You've given yourself another shot by taking some good, physical strides to dispose of stuff. The opening means you can get creative with all the thoughts you had for yourself. You're left with nothing but you, without all the outside and leftover weights to attempt and hold fast to.

Less Stress

Clutter powers your mind to take a shot at overdrive practically all the time. Continually contending with others puts your feeling of self in the things you can manage the cost of rather than in your identity. Having old things frequently hanging around you makes you consider all the objectives you had that you have forgotten, even if they were never really a big objective.

Disposing of all those weights, letting your cerebrum unwind, and dispensing with the fanciful challenge all indicates one major thing: You'll have less pressure. You'll still have some worry, obviously, yet your benchmark feelings of anxiety will drop, and you'll have the capacity to deal with the intense stressors all the more proficiently.

More Money for Experiences

One of the critical parts of enduring happiness is spending your cash on encounters rather than things. Purchasing items may give you momentary satisfaction, yet that doesn't last. Instead, that thing you got tends to wind up some portion of the foundation before long. In a year, you'll get nothing out of that thing.

Purchasing an experience is altogether extraordinary. Every time you recollect what you did or you take a gander at pictures from your excursion, you'll feel similar happiness about the adventure for quite a long time. Whenever you need to purchase presents for a vacation, avoid the endowments. Travel instead, even if it's a short one that is up close and personal. You and your family will love the switch and will become closer.

Moderation isn't merely something you ought to do because it looks cool. It's an incredible objective to support your mental health and wellbeing. It can enable you to find out about the things you need rather than the things you want, and it can allow you to feed your associations with others. All people need great social help, and attempting to keep yourself mentally fit is one of the initial phases in getting that.

CHAPTER TWO

Why We Should Embrace a Minimalist Lifestyle

When you consider somebody is carrying on with a minimalist lifestyle, what rings a bell? Are you living in some small shack out in the forested areas with no power while developing your very own nourishment and wearing the latest lumberjack fashions?

The small miracle is you've not to endeavored to investigate it further. That sort of life doesn't sound very engaging or straightforward. Fortunately, that is not actually what the minimalist lifestyle is about. Somewhat, it's tied in with returning to the reality of your identity.

It's tied in with living with only what you need, what you like, and what you use. It means letting the rest go. It's about never again hanging onto things, individuals, or exercises you don't appreciate because you generally have had them in your life.

It's about intentionally carrying on with a progressively simple lifestyle that allows for increased happiness, health, and efficiency – or at any rate, less turmoil and dramatization.

There is no single way to achieve and keep up a minimalist lifestyle; it's progressively about encircling yourself with ONLY what you need to fulfill your life and health.

What that means is up to you. However, numerous individuals, who are pulled in to the minimalist lifestyle, battle with how to start unraveling themselves from a lifetime of clutter.

Thankfully, that battle can end today.

Here are some approaches to begin along the path to a minimalist lifestyle:

1. Have Less Clutter:

Numerous individuals understand that one of the countless advantages that originate from carrying on with a minimalist lifestyle is that you have far less clutter. The minimalist lifestyle asks you to live with what you genuinely use, need, and appreciate in your life.

Did you realize that less clutter can likewise mean:

- Less real confusion means less earth, dust, form, buildup, and concealed bug pervasions.
- Less passionate clutter means you rest better, are more focused, and feel more liberated to settle on your own decisions without blame, dread, or disgrace blurring your judgment.

- Less profound clutter means, after time, you settle on self-cherishing decisions and experience your most joyful, healthiest and most productive life.

- Whenever you keep things in your home, vehicle, office, and life that holds no importance – or more regrettable are notices of unsavory recollections – it keeps you down. Your clutter is preventing you from feeling more joyful, healthier, and increasingly productive.

- The more you stick to things that aren't vital in your life, the more troublesome it will be to work well throughout everyday life.

- Go moderate and let go of anything you don't like, use, or need. Before long, you'll discover a great deal of room, time, and openings opening up to you.

2. Increment Your Happiness:

Having clutter means settling on more choices (even if that choice is to keep away from the confusion and pretend it is not there). That usually prompts pressure, overwhelming feelings, and weariness. Fortunately for you, carrying on with a minimalist lifestyle causes you to feel more joyful and reduce your feelings of anxiety.

Here's the ticket:

- Less clutter means fewer obligations. Just keep work, errands, and exercises that will enable you to remain or wind up cheerful, healthy, and productive.
- Increased efficiency means that you quit concentrating on the diversions because there are none. You're accomplishing more in less time. What's more, it feels great.
- Individual strength means you're responsible for your central leadership as opposed to allowing exercises, individuals, work, or errands to make your decisions for you.
- The more you let go of everything that isn't completely important in life, regardless of whether that is the stuff, the duties – and even the passionate garbage we as a whole tend to clutch – the more comfortable life feels.
- The more comfortable life feels, the more natural life gets because we've decided to concentrate on our needs.

3. Appreciate Extra Time:

At the point when your life looks and feels crazy, you think the time is continually neutralizing you. You feel like you do not influence your own life. Those carrying on with a minimalist lifestyle realize that their time is valuable and that they must fare thee well and oversee it legitimately.

Here's the way they do it:

- **Realize you're in charge:** The more you understand that you – and just you – have authority over HOW you spend your time, the more extra errands and things you can dispose of from your life.
- **Rundown your needs:** Next, set normal limits to guarantee you can keep centered, even if life tosses a few challenges at you.
- **Get enough rest:** You lose time, and you don't think well when you're tired. So the more well-rested you are, the more productive, more joyful, and decisive you'll be.
- You have much more authority over your own time if you essentially be mindful of how you're spending it.
- When you can recognize which exercises are deserving of your time and vitality, you can keep them while re-appropriating, designating, or essentially dropping undesirable practices.

Keep in mind: it's your decision.

4. Experience More Space:

The more clutter you dispose of, the more space you will appreciate. Space allows you to inhale, move, and think better. Lifestyle minimalists understand this, and now you can, as well.

Here's the ticket:

Just hang what must be hung in your storerooms. Increment your space by putting everything else in drawers.

Begin by dealing with the "simple" classifications first, like your clothing. At that point, hold up until the end to begin assessing the passionate and harder things, such as photographs and memorabilia. This makes the procedure snappier and easier.

Crease your clothing into square shapes, and after that, place them vertically as opposed to horizontally. This will empower you to observe and get anything rapidly. This strategy will likewise build your rack space by up to 50 percent.

If you're battling under your clutter to discover space, head out into nature and merely take a couple of minutes to inhale and value the absence of stuff. Imagine what your home would resemble without all that. At that point, head back home to change your space into your perception.

You'll additionally discover greater clearness with space, as clutter causes overwhelm and diversion.

5. Live Healthier:

Researchers are finding that clutter is causing many more health issues than anybody imagined. It's not merely some additional sniffling because of soil and residue. Your stuff can be causing anxiety, sadness, inadequate rest, and asthma and weight increase, to give some examples.

Some portion of the minimalist lifestyle is concentrating on health as a need. Here's the secret:

- Improve your nature of rest by expelling administrative work and hardware from your room.
- Reduce anxiety and disappointment by searching for simple approaches to set up straightforward frameworks, for example, setting a bowl close to your door to hold your keys.
- Put aside a couple of minutes in your timetable to incorporate exercise. Even light exercise like strolling can reduce anxiety and stress. It will likewise enable you to get in shape and rest better.
- Healthy living isn't just about eating a couple of carrots once in a while. It is a way of life that

should be kept up every single day. The less you have burdening you, the easier it is to remain healthy.

6. Assemble Stronger Relationships:

The individuals who have converted to carrying on with a minimalist lifestyle have revealed feeling that their associations with everyone have become more grounded and that their emotionally supportive network has improved.

Here's the reason:

- **Quality over amount:** Fewer friends mean more opportunity to develop more grounded associations with the friends who support you as much as you're supporting them.
- **Liberated to act naturally:** Quality friendships allow individuals to move naturally, which means they never again feel the need to spend time and energy looking after friendships.
- **Less mayhem:** Cutting free connections that are unhealthy, unsupportive, debilitating, or overwhelming encourages you to appreciate and participate in a protected and supportive condition.

Negative or riotous connections are as harmful to an individual's happiness, health, and profitability as physical clutter. The more we center on healthy, glad, supportive relationships, and the less we focus on what number of "friends" we have, the better relationships we'll appreciate.

7. More Money:

A minimalist lifestyle means you're compelled to settle on intelligent choices on how you spend your cash – because there's less space to keep stuff in. The moderate way of life implies there's less reliance on material satisfaction and more dependence on YOU fulfilling yourself.

So this means:

- Less stuff means fewer bills to pay and monitor.
- Purchasing just what you need means eliminating rash buys and additional waste.
- More comfortable to monitor funds, and you're more reluctant to lose cash in arbitrary spots.

Why Most Highly Productive And Successful People Are Minimalists

10 Benefits of minimalism (why toning it down would be best)

1. Opportunity from commercialization

A minimalist lifestyle can assist you with freeing yourself from the sturdy handle material possessions apply on your life. By figuring out how to acknowledge what you have, you turn out to be increasingly content with your general life. Minimalism establishes the framework for craving less while being more joyful with less. A minimalist lifestyle resembles the freedom from the abundances of industrialism. What's more, by beating the consumerist mentality, a significant advance towards an increasingly rearranged and meaningful life can be made.

2. Higher focus on the basics

Minimalist living does not suggest that you need to give away everything you own. Instead, it intends to divert your focus on that which is fundamental by relinquishing everything that doesn't increase the value of your life. It wants to de-clutter your life by flipping it around and shaking it tenderly. The possessions, exercises, and people that are imperative to you will stick. Everything of practically no significance will be washed away. The outcome is mental clarity and significant serenity.

It will likewise assist you with spending less time stressing over things that are not essential to you.

3. Mental clarity

When you let go of distracting things that add nothing but mental clamor to your life, you gain a higher dimension of mental clarity. It's a unique benefit of a minimalist lifestyle that one is less busy with endeavoring to acquire material possessions. Rather than owning many distracting things, you have less but increasingly meaningful things. To put it plainly, minimalism keeps your life clutter free and encourages you to build clarity of mind. Mental clarity thus empowers you to focus more on the things that add value and happiness to your life.

4. Less pressure

Minimalists are comfortable with less. A considerable extent of their happiness originates from the capacity to draw joy and satisfaction from a simple life. They have understood that the quest for more does not naturally prompt a meaningful existence. Thus, they never again feel the need to twist around in reverse to keep attempting to satisfy wants that are unquenchable.

When you are increasingly comfortable with having less, you will be less disposed to seek after a calling that you detest to get enough money, so you can acquire material possessions you don't need. This can significantly diminish pressure. You'll have substantially less to stress over, which causes you to be progressively aware of things and exercises you genuinely appreciate.

5. Gratefulness for the seemingly insignificant details in life

The minimalist mentality will assist you with understanding that you, as of now, have everything you need to be glad. Happiness is a decision and must be found inside. That is the motivation behind why incredibly rich people can be just as miserable, troubled, and unfulfilled as poor or white-collar class people. Nothing outer can ever add to your long-term happiness.

Carrying on with a minimalist lifestyle makes you increasingly energetic about the easily overlooked details in life. Typically, these are the superbly delightful things, yet to a great extent, disregarded. People nowadays are intensely involved in pursuing more, so they have great trouble welcoming the miracles and delights of their present lives. Instead, they underestimate these things, which makes it unbelievably hard to feel thankful for these little things.

6. Purpose and significance

Where it counts, we realize that commercialization does not genuinely fulfill us. We comprehend that everything it does is to enable us to satisfy a portion of our wants. It doesn't include the feeling of having a purpose. If a person draws meaning from the negligible obtaining and accumulation of material effects, they probably won't experience a meaningful existence.

A minimalist lifestyle is, to a great extent, focused on the capacity to recognize and welcome the essential and excellent perspectives in your life. It encourages you to control every one of your activities towards a progressively meaningful existence. As a minimalist, you're less likely in an unacceptable profession that you seek after for the money. Instead, minimalism gives you the chance to try a calling that adds purpose and importance to your life.

7. Additional time

The minimalist lifestyle accompanies the great benefit of having additional time. Not exclusively will you invest less energy with every one of the exercises important to acquire material possessions, and you will spend less time with activities or people that are not meaningful to you. You may never again feel the need to sit in front of the TV for a considerable length of time or praise the birthday of somebody you don't know or like. Furthermore, that is the genuine excellence of carrying on with a minimalist life. It's not tied in with relinquishing things that you hold dear or denying yourself certain encounters. Minimalism is tied in with accounting for the extraordinarily vital and meaningful parts of life.

8. Extra money

It shocks no one that you will naturally purchase substantially less when you want less. In this sense, minimalism is an excellent method for setting aside some cash. It will urge you to spend less money buying a significant number of things with next to zero value for your life. Subsequently, you set aside some cash, and a portion of this extra money can be utilized to purchase items of a higher quality that increase the value of your life.

9. Less correlation

Another great benefit of a minimalist lifestyle is that it puts a conclusion to the correlation amusement. Meanwhile, you don't have to keep contrasting yourself and the riches or material achievements of other people if you don't want these things. With minimalism comes the acknowledgment that correlations are quite often vile. It's inherently difficult to contrast the achievements of your life and those of someone else. A simple lifestyle does not require associations. You'll feel comfortable with what you have, and you'll be okay with the idea that others have significantly more (material) things. Furthermore, when you quit contrasting yourself with other people, you free yourself from the unhappiness and discontent that accompanies uncalled for examinations.

10. Less terrified of disappointment

You'll be progressively under strain when much is in question. In the meantime, if you have a lot to lose, you will be much more scared of a disappointment than somebody who does not have anything to lose. If you don't need to pay $2000 per month for an extreme level and another $800 for a decent car, you'll be less spooked by the dread of losing everything. Minimalists don't have a lot to lose and can be splendidly content with having nothing more than the minimum necessities.

Minimalist lifestyle tips

Here are some essential tips for you if you are considering living a more minimalistic or simplistic life:

- **Begin with an evaluation of your life.** Discover what precisely you're investing your energy and money on and assess if this is fundamental or justified, despite all the trouble. Usually, people have a wide range of budgetary responsibilities that are not critical in any case. In the meantime, they spend a great arrangement of their time with distracting exercises of no apparent value. Check whether you can lessen the time and money you pay in an insignificant and unfulfilling way.

- **Find what is extremely imperative.** At the foundation of a minimalist lifestyle lies the capacity to find and appreciate what is hugely critical to you. It's in this manner of great significance to build a conventional understanding of your needs. By comprehending what is vital, you will be better ready to focus on the quest for the parts of your life that are of genuine value to you.

- **Dispose of time-squandering exercises.** We know the activities that do nothing but squander our time. A portion of these exercises are genuinely engaging, yet they don't include much value. Have the bravery to name these exercises as what they are and to dispose of them from your life. You will see that you increase substantially more than you surrender.

- **Relinquish the things you will never need.** Don't merely keep things because you appreciated utilizing them ten years ago. De-clutter your life from everything that you don't need.

Significantly more vitally, dispose of each one of those things that don't increase the value of your life.

- **Dispose of bad connections.** A few people are inherently harmful. They harm you with their negative frame of mind, control you to make their offering, or channel your vitality. Despite what they do, when you feel a person has a very contrary effect on your life, consider giving the relationship a chance to end.

- **Focus more on timeliness.** Whatever choice you meet, check whether there is an increasingly timeless or adaptable alternative. It's not generally a great plan to base your buying choices principally dependent on most recent (design) patterns. In the meantime, focus on purchasing things that are of a higher quality that will last any longer.

- **Dispense with diversions.** If your consideration is routinely upset by standard electronic warnings or different sorts of distractions, check whether you can dispose of them. Nobody needs warnings from Facebook and Twitter. All they do is divert you from focusing on what is essential.

What Minimalism Could Mean for Your Career

Set aside the effort to investigate your interests and choose if your present career path feels right. Investigate outsourcing as an afterthought to experiment with various kinds of work, or volunteer to help a cause that you care firmly about. If your job is leaving you depleted, so it appears as though there's no extra time for these different interests, this could be a sign that things are unsustainable.

Expand Less, Live More

Here's a calming measurement: around 62 percent of Americans are living paycheck to paycheck. That implies they have no rainy day account if a vehicle needs repairing, a rooftop begins leaking, or some other sudden cost happens. With such an absence of money related security – paying little mind to salary level – it can appear to be challenging to make a stride back and glance around for work that may compensate in manners past your wallet.

To give yourself a superior possibility of seeking after the most critical career, it bodes well to make some financial breathing room. Separate needs from wants with regards to new buys and save somewhere around 10 percent of each check. Being predictable with this after some time will bear the cost of your alternatives with regards to getting another line of work or wandering down a new career path.

Reassess Regularly

While quite a bit of moderation revolves around restricting the gathering of superfluous material belongings, the idea can be summed up to each aspect of life – including your career. At normal interims, take an accurate account of where you are and if it's the place you need to be. Comprehend that what you may look for from a job will change after some time, as conditions develop and needs modify.

If you find that, after some time, your present title, pay or organization has left you disappointed, make a move. Regardless of whether it's refreshing abilities, consulting for better pay, or putting resources into your system, be proactive, so you don't stall out in work that feels useless or unchallenging.

The 10 Most Lucrative Minimalist Careers
1. Freelance Copywriter

- Average Earnings: $63,280
- Top 10% Earnings: $100,910+

Copywriters are writers that compose content, frequently for online productions and promoting. Numerous copywriters are freelance writers, and any-thing with the word freelance before it is profoundly adaptable because you make your calendar. There are higher dangers as an independent essayist. However, the prizes are remarkable – as a freelance writer, you can work from any area with wifi, pick whatever hours you need, and set your compensation grade. You must be great. Similarly, as a specialist, sales rep, or some other expert makes opportunity through his client base, you must most likely form a strong reputation among your clients — more from bls.gov.

2. Statistician Consultant

- Average Earnings: $95,980
- Top 10% Earnings: $160,000+

If you cherish numbers and insights, this may be the perfect job for you. Statisticians work with busi-nesses as their clients, breaking down their monetary expenses of risk. They can estimate and enable com-panies to create strategies that limit money related to risk. This career is an incredible minimalist decision due to the dimension of flexibility you can achieve as an expert. The drawback: To assemble a client base, it requires investment, and it very well may be anything but challenging to exhaust yourself in the first place. All around arranged execution can limit the risk of poor needs in any case.

3. Freelance Web Professional

- Average Earnings: $73,830
- Top 10% Earnings: $115,660+

Website admins and other web experts are in progressively extreme interest, and the result is excellent. Rewarding pay and, like some other freelancers, opportunity in each class. In any case, once more, it accompanies risks, and you must be great.

4. Specialist, Sole Practitioner

- Average Earnings: $166,400
- Top 10% Earnings: $356,885+

This career is not quite the same as different careers that require their very own training to be a minimalist career. The more clients you get, the greater flexibility (and typically cash) you win. Contingent upon the exercise, you can transform your job as a specialist into an exceptionally worthwhile and adaptable one preceding turning into a sole practitioner, even though ultimate rewards in the minimalist field are as yet holding up at that end. Like the legal counselor, the principal drawback is time and cash spent on school — more from bls.gov.

5. Dental practitioner, Sole Practitioner

- Average Earnings: $146,920
- Top 10% Earnings: $166,400+

There's a great deal of crossover in the therapeutic careers. As a dental practitioner, there's a great deal of time and cash required toward the front, which dependably implies massive amounts of understudy advances. That is the minimalist's bad dream, so do your best to maintain a strategic distance from as much of it as you can, utilizing stipends, understudy help, and grants — more from bls.gov.

6. Sales Rep

- Average Earnings: $46,770
- Top 10% Earnings: $115,340+

Finally, a high potential career that doesn't require an indecent measure of instruction. Sales careers are commonly very intuitive – you will have it, or you don't. In case you're great with individuals and appreciate conveying admirably, you'll likely need to test your abilities in sales. The minimalist factor in sales careers is of intense interest. The businesses that offer exceedingly adaptable sales jobs can be elusive, unless you're willing to work off of general commission; however, in case you're great, it's not a big issue. More from bls.gov.

7. Individual Financial Adviser

- Average Earnings: $64,750
- Top 10% Earnings:$166,400+

What a few people may not understand is that their own money related consultants are, in reality, merely proficient sales reps. They "deal with" individuals' cash by "exhorting" their organization's stocks, securities, shared assets, retirement plans, and other money-related administrations. HR supervisors search for sales ability most importantly. The flexibility is typically very high, albeit numerous individuals wind up working long hours to remain focused — more from bls.gov.

8. CPA, Sole Practitioner

- Average Earnings: $61,690
- Top 10% Earnings: $106,880+

The CPA made the rundown in light of the chance to end up as a sole practitioner. Bookkeepers that work for organizations have incredible hours contrasted with most business experts. However, their flexibility is restricted. To seek a minimalist career in this market, the main course is to end up as a CPA and begin your very own training — more from bls.gov.

9. Attorney, Sole Practitioner

- Average Earnings: $112,760
- Top 10% Earnings: $166,400+

Once more, a career that is only minimalist if you turn into a sole practitioner. The voyage is long and hard. However, the advantages are considerable. The drawbacks are 7-8 years of school and a profoundly focused career path. In case you're sure about your capacities and comprehend that disappointment is the venturing stone to progress, you'll make it. Turning into a legal advisor is just the start. Making it a moderate profession is another long and exhausting voyage. To those ready to forfeit the time and apply a superhuman exertion, it's sure to be justified even despite the hardship — more from bls.gov.

10. Real estate agent

- Average Earnings: $42,680
- Top 10% Earnings: $95,220+

Like the budgetary guide, real estate brokers are sales operators with a superior reputation to the run of the mill deals rep. They get paid commission from the houses they sell, so it's to their most significant advantage to produce a quick turnaround for the most noteworthy dollar. The job offers a lot of flexibility, particularly if you run your own office. The critical step is, as a rule, sufficient – you must be an incredible communicator with a lot of sales ability.

8 Ways Minimalism Can Help Your Finances

Minimalism is a development that focuses on decreasing the messiness in your life, both in physical articles and in different diversions. People who grasp it find ways to dispose of the distractions from their lives, and it opens more doors for them in different ways and zones. Grasping minimalism does not imply that you quit spending money. However, it can mean that you spend it on different things, and your focus may change from profiting to getting a charge out of life. Here are ten ways minimalism can support your finances.

Enables You to Prioritize Your Spending

Minimalism urges you to grasp the things that are most critical to you. This will typically persist in how you spend your money. If you are not focused on obtaining certain items but rather progressively focused on explicit encounters, the way you spend your money changes. Acknowledging what is most critical to you will help with your spending needs, and this can convey the idea that you handle your money by and large.

Limits the Need for Things

When you are concentrating on moderation, you are regularly restricting what you possess. Since you claim less or spend less on buying items, it can support you if you need to curtail your spending to build your funds or to escape debt. Frequently, since you are not buying as much, you can put more money towards other financial goals that can enable you to focus on encounters as opposed to things. This may mean early retirement or a better get-away.

You Need Less Room (Save on Mortgage or Rent)

When you are rehearsing moderation, you need less space to store everything that you have gathered throughout the years. When you buy or lease a little space, you can save money on the lease. However, you can even have a decent home with clean lines and an area that you cherish. As you get out a portion of your things, you may find that you can set aside extra cash by moving to a little spot. Not exclusively, this will save you on your lease or home loan, and it can save you on utilities and free up much more money to spend on the things that are most vital to you.

Gives You Focus When It Comes to Financial Goals and Budget

Moderation is tied in with practicing care in your life. This can profit you as you start planning and defining your financial goals. Planning is a spending plan dependent on your present needs. As you find what is most essential to you, it becomes easier to choose when and how to spend your money. It can likewise enable you to see places where you need to change the way you handle your money like the amount that you pay in premium every month on different credits.

Concentrate on Getting Out of Debt and Living Debt Free

One approach to rearranging your finances is to focus on escaping debt. Numerous people start by squaring away their purchaser debt and, after that, decide to have a charge card to deal with crises. Disposing of debt opens various entryways and gives you the freedom to leave an occupation that you don't care for or remove a year to travel. If you don't have other regularly scheduled installments, it is a lot easier to investigate and do the things that are the most vital to you.

Consider Selling Items as You Free Yourself of Them

If you are merely starting to grasp minimalism, you can sell the items you don't want or need. You can utilize this money to enable you to begin to clear up the financial mess in your life, similar to your debt. The funds can likewise go to kick off a rainy day account or to support an excursion that you have always needed to take. As you free yourself of the messiness in your life, you can go through the money to clear your financial slip-ups as well. Holding a yard sale is a simple way to sell many items rapidly.

Causes You to Find Ways to Simplify Your Finances

There are a few things you can do to make taking care of your funds less demanding. You can pay your bills all in one day. You can change to money for consistent buys, which makes following you're spending easier. You may likewise need to find an application that streamlines the planning procedure. If you see a portable app that works for you, you can enter buys in a hurry and know where you are with your goals and breaking points.

Makes Giving Easier

When you comprehend what is most essential and have your finances leveled out, it can make giving back less demanding. This means giving back in time or giving back through gifts. When you are practicing minimalism, it is anything but painful to perceive what you can give and the amount you can provide. It makes moving your needs easier when needed.

CHAPTER THREE

How Minimalism Can Improve Your Finances

Minimalism and your finances

Minimalism can have an immensely positive effect on your finances with regards to getting out of debt, setting aside some cash, and building wealth. Having a minimalistic approach can enable you to achieve your financial goals quicker and improve your demeanor as you experience the way toward creating wealth. Let's talk through precisely how minimalism can improve your finances.

1. Minimalism can enable you to pick up lucidity around your core values

Like I referenced above, minimalism is tied in with relinquishing what doesn't make a difference in your life and focusing on what does. The things that matter to you will regularly spin around your core values that, once you distinguish, can assist you with the procedure of disposal (having less) and adopting a more minimalistic strategy to your life.

For example, if you want to travel, but you find yourself spending thoughtless hours in the shopping center buying things you needn't bother with, you can, preferably, start putting those extra assets into a movement account towards the movement encounters that will satisfy you.

If giving back and helping other people is something that genuinely satisfies you but your storage room is blasting at the creases with garments you've never worn, scarcely wear, and don't generally like, you can give back by giving those garments to people who need or want them.

If you haven't as of now, try distinguishing your core values by putting forth these inquiries - 1) What are the things and encounters that genuinely matter to you? Also, 2) when you take a gander at how you spend your money today, does your spending line up with those values?

2. Minimalism means buying less, which means spending less

Numerous people can't help disagreeing concerning this point since buying less does not really mean spending less but listen to me here.

Many times, people buy things because they are shabby, and it appears to be a grand bargain. In any case, since they are so shabby or such an ambitious deal, they end up buying an ever increasing number of things they don't generally need and may not like. What's more, rather than focusing on their core values (the things that matter), at that point, it turns into a focus on the following deal and the next bargain and the next great reasonable outfit and so forth.

They end up spending more money, not less, on things that are not lined up with their core values and don't acquire them much fulfillment in the long run. So yes, in numerous cases, buying less means spending less, which means more money in your pocket to pay debt, save, and contribute.

3. Minimalism enables you to focus on satisfying your debt quicker

Following the past point, buying less means having more money to put towards things that matter to you, like escaping debt, and the more money you put against your mortgage, the speedier you can leave the debt cycle and begin putting a more significant amount of your money towards your financial and life goals. It's a win-win approach - buy less, have more, pay off debt, and manufacture wealth.

4. Minimalism brings genuine feelings of serenity and satisfaction

Genuine feelings of serenity and satisfaction are a side-effect of a moderate's lifestyle. The decrease of messiness and careless spending can take out pressure, and because you are just spending money on the things that genuinely bring you bliss, you will have a great feeling of joy and satisfaction. You don't need to stress over putting away or keeping up or notwithstanding paying for things you don't even genuinely need.

6 Popular Minimalist DE cluttering Methods

1. KonMari Method

Fundamentals: The core rule of the KonMari method is that, as opposed to choosing what to dispose of, you pick what to keep and clean up the rest. To begin, gather every item you claim in a specific classification and place them in a major heap. For instance, get each shirt that you possess and put them on the bed. Hold, feel, or wear every one with the goal that you can get a decent feeling of how it affects you. While doing this, inquire:

Does this (shirt) flash delight in my heart?

Geniuses: This decluttering method is unbelievably intensive and enables you to think about all items of a comparable sort. By doing this, you can dispose of any copies and think about well-worn, less-loved items to more up to date and better ones you may have. It's a powerful way to gain a ton of ground decluttering in explicit classifications over various zones of the house on the double.

Cons: The KonMari method is time-consuming and requires dealing with a whole family unit of stuff. Rather than focusing on a room or two, you're pulling things from the entire house, so it can evacuate your home.

2. Moderate Game

Fundamentals: Beginning on the first day of a month, the quantity of things you clean up relates to the day of the month. One item on the first day, two articles on the second day, three on the third, etc. Before the end of a 31-day month, you will have expelled 496 items from your home if you play entirely through. This amusement works best when you challenge a companion or relative and see who can keep up the longest.

Professionals: After a month, you will have cleaned up a vast amount of stuff! Expelling very nearly 500 items from your home is no little accomplishment, and you can play the same number of months in succession as you'd like. Another essential part of this decluttering method is that it begins little and increments a little at a time. This enables you to fabricate confidence in your important leadership capacities and show signs of improvement relinquishing stuff.

Cons: A noteworthy drawback of the minigame is that you need to remain consistent every day; generally, it's easy to fall behind. Much like Tetris, the trouble expands each dimension, and it very well may be hard to keep up unless you're staying aware of the pace. Towards the month's end, it can likewise be overpowering. The exact opposite thing you should need to do in the wake of returning home from a stressful day of work is to find 25 items to clean up that day.

3. Four Box Method

This method is a flexible way to manage every one of the items jumbling up your home and whatever recurrence you incline toward. By arranging the messiness into four classifications, you'll settle on a choice on each item.

Nuts and bolts: Set up four boxes in a room and name them: Put away, Give away, Throw away, and undecided. Get the mess in the place and put it into one of the four boxes, and after that, deal with each box as indicated by the name. This form takes into consideration some adaptability by utilizing the Undecided table in case you don't know how to manage a specific item yet. Another variety of this method without the Undecided box can be found from Joshua Becker on Becoming Minimalist.

Experts: This decluttering method is direct, and there's a classification for everything. As opposed to stalling out on an item you don't know whether you need to dispose of, things in the Undecided box can be reconsidered at some future date. It enables you to be adaptable and clean up at your very own pace.

Cons: The Undecided box can turn into an issue if a large number of things begin to heap up in it. It's ideal for abstaining from utilizing this box however much as could reasonably be expected and just put in stuff you're incredibly uncertain about.

4. One Method

Rudiments: This method was made by combining other comparable rationalities into a straightforward concept: dispose of one thing every day for a timeframe. That thing can be one item, one filled box, or one filled sack for each day.

Geniuses: The One Method constructs a propensity for decluttering. By disposing of a sum every day, you're ready to incorporate decluttering with your day by day schedule. Another significant advantage is the adaptability to make your very own framework.

You can pick your dimension for every day, relying upon the amount you need to clean up.

Cons: Due to the consistency required for this technique, it might be hard to stay aware of a bustling calendar or if you have timeframes when you're away from home. This method likewise wouldn't function admirably for somebody who likes to work in substantial fiery blasts instead of little advances every day.

5. Pressing Party

Another method from The Minimalists, this is a genuinely excellent method for decluttering your home and bound to be utilized if you're anticipating moving to another house. While it takes a tremendous amount of readiness and work (you might need to enroll the assistance of your companions), it very well may be mighty if you proceed with it.

Fundamentals: Have a few companions over and pack everything you claim into boxes as though you were moving. Throughout the following couple of months, take out the items you use. After around three months, the things left inside the boxes are sold or given away.

Stars: As a standout amongst the most extraordinary and work severe decluttering methods, the Packing Party will enable you to dispose of whatever you don't utilize. Things out of sight will, in general, be out of mind too, so you likely won't miss the items stashed in the boxes. This method is fantastic if you happen to move. Merely take the boxes to your new home and take out the things you use as opposed to unloading everything immediately.

Cons: This method presumably doesn't bode well unless you are getting ready for a move. And it will require a lot of investment and vitality. There's likewise the expense of acquiring boxes if you don't have them. This method also doesn't function admirably for regular items or items just utilized two or three times per year.

6. Storage room Hanger Method

Oprah pointed out a great deal of these methods as another compelling way to make sense of what clothing and different items you use. The Closet Hanger method enables you to follow precisely what's been utilized without utilizing a tremendous exertion like the pressing party.

Rudiments: Per the name, this works best to put away clothes on holders in your storeroom (duh). While it works best to confront the holders another way, the most important thing is to guarantee all holders are facing a similar course when you start. As you wear items of clothing every day, you place them back in the storage room with the holder looking the opposite way to show what you wore.

Aces: This DE-cluttering method is anything but challenging to actualize and sets aside no effort to begin. It's likewise an obvious way to see precisely what you're utilizing and what you're most certainly not. A similar method can be connected to things outside of clothing, yet you'll need to concoct a way to check what items are utilized.

Cons: Specifically to dress, the Closet Hanger method doesn't function for folded pieces in a cabinet or on a rack. Control is needed to put the clothing item back on the holder facing the proper way to have a reasonable picture toward the end of the time outline. For things outside of clothing, it might be hard to make sense of a framework to figure out what you use versus what you don't. Like the Packing Party method, this method doesn't function admirably for random or rarely utilized items.

8 Top Minimalist Living Tips

1. Assess and inspect

An essential piece of carrying on with a minimalist life sees your material possessions with a goal focal point. Experience every part of your life, your home, and your lifestyle. The initial step is trustworthiness, ruthless genuineness. You need to see where you can decrease and what you can live without.

This is frequently the hardest stage. However, the good news is that, once you've done this, the rest will come effectively. Thus, accumulate an agenda and see where you can cut expenses and dispose of items. For instance, is your storeroom flooding, yet you wear around six outfits? Do you spend a good 30 minutes endeavoring to discover a lid for your plastic holders? Soliciting these sorts of inquiries will make the process a lot less demanding and will likewise assist you with evaluating and inspecting somewhat more effectively.

2. Clean up

Experience each room in your house, your vehicle, and even your work area at work. Begin by disposing of copies; why have two when you have one—this is a minimalist living proverb.

Next, if you haven't used it in a half year, the chances are that you're not going to use or need it again at any point shortly, and it is doing you no good. If it isn't adding to your life or your bliss, throw it away. If there are terrible recollections connected, hurl it away.

3. Think before you buy

Financially plan your money. You've cleaned up your home, and you've gained extraordinary ground; however, at this point, you should remain on the steed. You can't circumvent buying everything you need. Minimalist living is about needs, not wants. Before purchasing something, ask yourself: How will this add to my life in one month? In one year?

If you can't think of a reason, it won't be a beneficial buy. An extraordinary thought is to experience your financial plan and see where you can cut $1,000, or if your assets are somewhat more restricted, $100. This may be a fun exercise that will result in you saving a ton of money.

Sparing somewhat all over can signify huge increases. Use the inspiration of buying something extraordinary like an occasion in a tear camper.

4. Buy quality

Try not to buy as often as possible; buy quality. If you need something, why not set something aside for the best quality? This will prevent you from excessive spending, and what you buy will keep going quite a while, implying that you should buy one item, and this will result in less mess.

Take a couple of shoes, for instance; set aside money consistently or monthly to buy a good pair of shoes. This means you will almost certainly wear them for more time and will need one set in your storage room rather than six.

5. Create appreciation

The more appreciative you are for the things you have, the more likely you will be progressively content. Check it out and discover happiness in the basic stuff. Search for excellence in the littlest of things and be content with what you have.

The more you buy, the more you need, and the more you are overwhelmed by getting things. That doesn't appear as though it would bring anybody satisfaction.

6. Cleanse

Rehash the cleaning up process frequently and no matter what. It is an unavoidable truth that, regardless of how hard we attempt, things begin to heap up, and it is dependent upon us to ensure that we don't slip into negative behavior patterns once more. Thus, don't worry. Make a point to clean up consistently.

This additionally means you explore new territory and energy, loosening up each at times. This is good for the psyche and the body. Life heaps on the pressure, and whether we know it or not, we are influenced by the weights we face each day.

In this way, cool off, unwind—you need it.

7. Don't blame yourself

Many of us cling to things because we feel remorseful. This means things we don't need, want or use are lounging around jumbling our minimalist lifestyle all because our auntie offered it to us. No more! State "no" to blame.

These things may have been given to us out of adoration, and we welcome the sentiment, yet we need to give it up. The time has come to give away and escape. Facilitate the blame by being straightforward— you're giving it a superior home. Presently, these items will be used and acknowledged rather than covered up and detested.

8. Try not to get attached to material belongings

The sad, unavoidable truth is that things occur. Sudden occasions and being in an unlucky spot means that material things get lost. They are split or stolen or removed all of a sudden. We need to be free of con-nection to material things when we need to proceed onward and embrace a minimalist lifestyle.

Along these lines, attempt this—give away some-thing new or that you genuinely love. Pick a home where it will be treasured, and you will have ventured out, giving up a connection to material belongings.

10 Minimalist Lifestyle Tips

Top tips to go for a minimalist lifestyle and how to live well with less.

1. Lesson

The best tip to live with less is to live with less. Evaluate your material possessions and figure out what you need and what you don't. An ideal approach to do this is to use the accompanying minimalist rules:

- Do I use this consistently?
- Does it profit?
- Do I completely cherish it?

When an item doesn't fall inside at least one of these, odds are you can live without it.

2. Reuse

Most items have a longer lifespan than our consumerist society would have you accept. Most can frequently be reused over and over. Also, buy things used. Give to used shops.

3. Reuse

Reuse everything you can! An ethical principle to remember is - If it's not recyclable, don't bring it into your life, because then it turns into your weight.

4. Upcycle

Upcycling realizes new possibilities for reusing. It's giving things another shot at life and transforming waste into fortune and turning garbage into craftsmanship and converting poo into inventiveness. As far as possible, upcycling is your creative ability.

5. Zero waste

Go for zero waste by remaining mindful of what items you bring into your reality. Make your very own consideration items. Avoid junk. If it's not reusable, recyclable, or compostable, you don't need it.

6. Compost

All original kitchen scraps can transform into soil-improving and plant-cherishing compost. Numerous urban areas overall offer compost pickup, and regularly there are building or neighborhood plants that cheerfully welcome compost. Or you can make your very own with a little compost receptacle and tumbler. Toss it in, forget about it; it mysteriously progresses toward becoming earth.

7. De-mess

In addition to the fact that clutter sucks, the simple nearness of messiness can cause mental pressure. It's an excess to look at, a lot for our cerebrums to process, and winds up overpowering and discouraging.

Effectively de-mess your life by handling one territory at a time until you are less messy or mess free. Your significant serenity will bless your heart.

8. Various use

Get items that can be used for various things or that can be used in different ways. Any article pulling twofold obligation spares you from buying extra things and decreases what you possess. For instance, a powerhouse multi-reason item, for example, a scarf can have more than 20 distinct uses.

9. Higher quality

Obtaining less gives you the advantage of acquiring higher quality items that last longer and don't need to be replaced. The quick style that is modest and simple isn't just contaminating the planet, and it's making you buy more since it needs to be replaced when it goes into disrepair.

10. Needless

Every one of these means a minimalist lifestyle adds to your general decrease in need and need for material goods. When you need less, you've beaten the framework! Commercials won't influence you any longer because you won't need that stuff. Moderation isn't tied in with making do with less; it's tied in with needing less.

CHAPTER FOUR

3 Psychological Benefits of Minimalism

Minimalism doesn't mean surrendering the vast majority of your common possessions and living out of a knapsack. You can possess a vehicle, have a rooftop over your head, utilize a couple of hardware, and keep more than one garment.

Minimalists pare down what they have. They take a gander at every possession and ask, "Do I truly require this? Truly?" They think about everything in the present setting, not whether it may be required in the future.

Some sell their homes and move into smaller houses. Others appreciate the additional room they make by having fewer possessions. In any case, minimalism brings more than living space. People get mental benefits from the lifestyle also.

Happiness

The outcomes are in: Money honestly doesn't buy happiness. An ongoing report discovered legal advisors who make the least money are the most joyful.

This mixed up relationship of money and happiness may make a few people battle for higher profit, trusting more money will get a more fulfilling life. Amusingly, this endeavor could come to the detriment of current happiness.

Other research demonstrates that encounters, not possessions, lead to enduring happiness. Delight starts when people plan and envision meetings, for example, excursions, shows, and trips. Fulfillment keeps amid the occasion, just as through later thinking back.

The purchase of articles does not bring comparable delight. Happiness blurs as people become accustomed to new possessions.

In reality, giving money away makes people more joyful. Another mental examination discovered people are more joyful when they burn through money on others as opposed to themselves. What's more, this outcome isn't influenced by people's salary levels.

More prominent Self-Esteem

Poor self-esteem is connected to materialism. The association shows up during puberty. As children move toward becoming adolescents, self-esteem will result in a general drop. In the meantime, materialism is on the ascent. Around the finish of secondary school, young people commonly feel better about themselves. In the meantime, their craving for possessions is disappearing.

Materialism doesn't influence only the youthful. Grown-ups who unknowingly have low dimensions of self-esteem will, in general, be progressively materialistic. The relationship goes both ways: Materialistic adults don't think a lot of themselves.

Regardless of whether they state they have an abnormal state of respect for themselves, it doesn't make any difference. It's what's happening under the surface that makes a distinction.

Less Stress

Everything is associated. Worldly people will, in general, have low self-esteem. What's more, these people regularly react to high stress by shopping, as the above investigation appears.

They purchase, wanting to feel better; however, the inverse happens. Imprudent spending prompts more stress.

To contemplate the connection between materialism and stress, specialists considered Israelis are living under extraordinary Palestinian rocket assaults for a half year. The greediest people were well on the way to take part in regular shopping and endure post-horrible stress.

A Little Minimalism

Minimalism isn't a surefire approach to end up mentally stable. There is merely an excessive number of outer and inner factors included. In any case, minimalism is related to benefits that assist people to live more joyful, increasingly fulfilled and more settled lives.

Also, you're not overwhelmed with clutter. That is both a superior headspace and an excellent living space.

6 Reasons Minimalism Will Improve Your Life

BENEFITS OF MINIMALISM

A modest lifestyle offers numerous benefits past merely being free of clutter. Minimalism gives mental and monetary benefits too!

1. Living with less stuff

The most evident benefit of minimalism is having less to clean, less to tidy, less to scour, and less stuff to secure every night. With fewer things to clean and arrange, you'll see it less demanding to keep your home clean.

2. Less Stress and Anxiety

There are mental benefits also. Do you feel like housework is never done? The worry of having an excessive amount to perfect, attempting to discover approaches to arrange everything, or merely the uneasiness from the absence of time to do everything. Farewell to the times of scouring Pinterest for sorting out thoughts.

Regardless of whether you are working or at home, having clutter in your life is exceptionally distracting. It can make you feel as if the world is surrounding you. You additionally increase your stress by not having the capacity to discover effectively the stuff you need.

3. All the more spare time

You won't invest energy scanning for answers to arranging your stuff. When was the last time you read a book, took a walk, or partook in your favorite hobby? Less stuff to think about equates more opportunity for you to do the things you cherish.

4. A greater spending plan

Owning stuff costs money, and we wind up caught in this cycle of commercialization. Continually purchasing more stuff that we don't generally require.

Instead, focus on what you need and the things that genuinely bring you delight. When you stop to assess purchases honestly, you may amaze yourself with what you can make do with.

5. Capacity to focus on the essential things

Rather than stressing over your assets, you are allowed to do what is most important to you. From investing energy with family, making the most of your favorite hobby, or offering back to your locale.

6. An alternate point of view

In this day of internet-based life, what every other person is doing is in our face day in and day out. We see our family, companions, neighbors, and colleagues flaunting their new house, excursion, or most recent device.

Keeping up with the Joneses prompts discontent. We center on what we don't have, what we are passing up, or what we wish we had.

Motivations to be moderate

Instead, focus on what you do have. Be thankful for the people and things in your life, rather than being desirous of others. By decreasing the measure of physical clutter, you can streamline your life!

What are the Benefits of a Minimalist Lifestyle?

It should not shock anyone that moderation is such an exciting issue nowadays. Our lives, while loaded up with more comforts than ever, are additionally more feverish than any other time in recent memory. Notwithstanding all that humanity has achieved so far, we find ourselves more stressed and with less free time than any other time. Fortunately, there's a simple fix that can fit into anyone's life. That is rehearsing moderation! In any case, what precisely would you be able to pick up from restraint? Here are the Benefits of a Minimalist Lifestyle!

1. Less Stress

Stress is the primary source of discontent in a great many people, so less weight is a standout amongst the best benefits of a minimalist lifestyle, as I would see it. A traditional consumerist lifestyle is stressful, what with every one of the things you continually have to purchase and do. In any case, a minimalist lifestyle spotlights on the essential elements. When your present PDA is as yet working fine, you don't need to mind that another adaptation just came out. What's more, being in your house is a stress-free affair, as you're not always endeavoring to revamp abundant things or see things that help you to re-member things you should/need to be doing.

2. More Money

Being a minimalist saves you money, mostly be-cause you understand you don't need to purchase that much. Minimalists don't stress over staying aware of the patterns in design or home stylistic lay-out. Minimalists additionally will, in general, have more vitality because their days are less saddling, so you'll see them spending less money eating out. Also, it's uncommon for them to make stress-related moti-vation buys.

3. Fewer Attachments

The more things you have, the more connections you have, the more stress you have. It's as simple as that. If you have a watercraft in your garage, you may stress that somebody is going to take your vessel. If you're taking your fresh out of the plastic new costly tablet to the bistro with you, you may stress over los-ing it. Also, an individual with a customary lifestyle has far more to be worried about losing if they see their security framework has been set off! While you'll gen-erally stress somewhat over the things you have, one of the benefits of moderation is that you can stress much less because you have significantly less stuff!

4. More Rest

Another of the numerous benefits of a minimalist lifestyle is more rest. That is because moderation incorporates disposing of exercises and assignments that aren't generally adding anything to your life. It's uncommon to find a minimalist spending an hour arranging mail that has been heaping up, and you won't see a minimalist taking a seat for a motion picture long distance race that they've chosen because of their pile of "to watch" DVDs was heaping up. Minimalists fill their lives with only the things they have to and would like to do, yet not that they feel they need to do (however truly don't need to). When you cut out the "need to dos," you'll find you have additional time, opening up the open door for perusing, snoozing, or heading to sleep on time.

5. Improved Relationships

When you're not spending all your time attempting to keep up with the Joneses or associating with every one of your things, you possess more energy for family and companions. You can be one of those families that has a table game night! Furthermore, you'll have room schedule-wise to call that companion you've been signed to make up for lost time with. So one of the significant benefits of moderation is having an increasingly dynamic and satisfying public activity!

6. Improved Health

Less stress, more grounded connections, more rest, and so forth all equates to a healthier life! The free time you gain from moderation alone could be a central point in improving your wellbeing. It can enable you to make home prepared dinners, invest energy working out, invest time outside getting vitamin D, and the sky is the limit from there. It's not uncommon to find people say they felt better and increasingly lively after only a month of minimalist living.

7. More Happiness

As anyone might expect, one of the benefits of a minimalist lifestyle is feeling more joyful. How would you be able to be more joyful with a more extravagant, freer, healthier life? Minimalists may encounter not so much dread but rather more certainty. The absence of fear originates from having less to lose if things go south (you could put additional time in a start-up when you don't have massive amounts of costs), and the expansion in certainty originates from figuring out how to approve of your identity and how your life is (and not continually contrasting yourself with others).

So, in general, a minimalist lifestyle gives you a freer, more joyful life where you can concentrate more on what you truly, really need to do with your time. It might be somewhat hard to begin changing your lifestyle to a minimalist one, yet with every one of these benefits, it merits the inconvenience!

7 Powerful Ways to Supercharge Your Life With Positivity

1. Peruse

Peruse books that move, support, and spur you on. It doesn't generally make a difference if you realize what the book is about. What makes a difference is that you ceaselessly feed your psyche with positive and rousing material. The additional time you can spend in the place that is known for the positive, the better. You increase the measure of time that you are sure. Also, when you continue doing this, you will, in the long run, become one of those glad, constructive people that can deal with any misfortune.

2. Tune in

The second thing I genuinely prefer to do when I'm going for a stroll, washing the dishes, or cleaning the house is to tune in to sound projects.

3. Core interest

While this may sound excessively oversimplified, a great many people don't do it, which is concentrate on the constructive as opposed to abiding upon the antagonistic. A great many people focus on current issues rather than the arrangements. It has been shown the majority of our stresses never at any point occur. That implies that you are stressing and making yourself feel stressed out for reasons unknown by any stretch of the imagination.

Next time you feel cynicism, please, flip it over and consider the positive part of it and what can be done. For instance, rather than asking, "Why me?" or "For what reason am I so unfortunate?" ask yourself, "What would I be able to gain from this?" and, "How might I turn this around?"

4. Discharge

There are some incredible approaches to discharging negative ideas and contrary convictions. A portion of my top picks is EFT, The Work, and Sedona Method. I suggest you attempt one of the strategies above. I truly appreciate working with EFT at present, which is short for Emotional Freedom Techniques. The greater pessimism you can discharge from your life, the more harmony you will feel inside and the more positive you will be.

5. Habits

What sort of habits do you have right now that cause antagonism in your life? What might your life look like if you began to change them? When we settle on the choice to break a habit, it nearly occurs without anyone else's input; however, you must be resolved to get it going.

As I said above, changing your musings resembles changing any habit in your life. It won't be simple, yet, on the other hand, feeling terrible all the time isn't a stroll in the park.

6. Goals

Most people never set any goals. I realize that it tends to be frightening to choose where you need to go, and you need to leave your alternatives open, yet nothing occurs until you get clear about where you need to go and what you need to do. It doesn't make a difference if your goals change. That is ordinary, and one reason you should continue tweaking your goals as the season's change.

A standout amongst the ideal approaches to set goals is to utilize the S.M.A.R.T criteria, which represents:

- Explicit
- Quantifiable
- Feasible
- Reasonable
- Timely

Your goals will give you center and reason, so ensure you set goals in every aspect of your life. The most widely recognized regions are wellbeing, connections, vocation, and self-awareness.

7. Enthusiasm

Do whatever it takes not to allow this to be you. Pursue your fantasies, regardless of whether it implies just having the capacity to set aside 10 minutes per day. If you begin today, you can expand upon what you have; however, if you continue putting it off, it will never occur.

Expanding the energy in your life is necessary, however painful. You need to assume liability and get it going because nobody will do it for you.

CONCLUSION

Minimalism depicts movements in art and configuration, film, writing, and music where the work is stripped down to its most essential and crude. Substance and structure are kept to the most shortsighted conceivable, trying to evacuate any sign of individual articulation. By paring down materials, compositions and methods, minimalists wish to touch base at the very wellspring of art before ages of artists altered it.

Minimalists expect to enable the watcher to encounter their work all the more seriously without the diversions of the considerable number of traditions, set manners of thinking, and proverbial images that barrage and stifle the human personality. It is established in the reductive aspects of Modernism and is regularly deciphered as a reaction against Abstract Expressionism and a scaffold to Post-present day art practices. Moderate Art rose in New York during the 1960s. It was viewed as a reaction against Abstract Expressionism, yet the artists in the movement disliked the tag of moderate and did not see their work as being part of a campaign by any means. However, they have joined in the idea that their art was not self-articulation. In spite of the fact that Minimalism disparaged the impact that artists had set on the virtue of art, they had spoils and implications in the geometric abstractions of painters in the Bauhaus, in the works of Piet Mondrian and different artists related with the movement DeStijl, in Russian Constructivists and is crafted by the Romanian stone worker Constantin Brancusi. So also to minimalism in art, artistic minimalism is described by toning it down, which would be an ideal mantra.